Guide to TensorFlow

Practical Guide

V. Telman

Copyright © 2024

Practical Guide

1. Introduction

TensorFlow is an open-source library developed by Google, used for machine learning and deep learning, with a particular focus on artificial neural networks. It is one of the most popular frameworks in the field of artificial intelligence (AI) due to its ability to handle large volumes of data and support the training and inference of deep learning models.

One of TensorFlow's main features is its flexibility: it can be used for a wide range of applications, from computer vision to speech recognition, natural language processing (NLP), and time series forecasting. TensorFlow enables developers to create machine learning models with a scalable architecture that can run on various types of platforms, from CPUs and GPUs to mobile devices.

TensorFlow aims to simplify the

development, training, and deployment of complex machine learning models while providing a solid foundation for advanced AI research. It uses a graph-based architecture, where data is represented as nodes and computations as edges, making it easy to optimize computational processes.

History and Development of TensorFlow

TensorFlow was developed by Google Brain, a research team at Google dedicated to artificial intelligence. Its first version was publicly released in November 2015 as an open-source project under the Apache 2.0 license. However, TensorFlow's roots go back to an internal Google project known as DistBelief, an early version of a distributed machine learning framework that Google had been using internally since 2011.

DistBelief was designed to handle large volumes of data and leverage Google's distributed computing infrastructure.

However, it had some limitations, especially in terms of flexibility and ease of use. TensorFlow was developed as an evolution of DistBelief, with the goal of making the framework more modular, flexible, and accessible to developers outside of Google.

Since 2015, TensorFlow has undergone numerous updates and improvements. One of the most significant releases was TensorFlow 2.0, released in September 2019. This version introduced a simpler and more intuitive interface, improved support for Keras, a high-level API for building and training deep learning models. Additionally, TensorFlow 2.0 removed some of the complexities of the earlier version, making the framework more accessible to newcomers while enhancing performance and scalability.

Key Milestones in TensorFlow Development:

- **2011**: Google begins using DistBelief as an internal framework for distributed learning.

- **2015**: Google releases TensorFlow as an open-source project.

- **2016**: TensorFlow becomes one of the most popular machine learning frameworks in the world.

- **2017**: Introduction of TensorFlow Lite, an optimized version for mobile devices.

- **2019**: Release of TensorFlow 2.0, with a simplified architecture and increased integration with Keras.

- **2020 and beyond**: TensorFlow continues to evolve with ongoing improvements, including optimizations for distributed computing and support for cloud computing platforms like TensorFlow Extended (TFX).

TensorFlow Architecture

TensorFlow has a modular architecture that allows for the execution of complex machine learning operations across different platforms, making the best use of available hardware resources. TensorFlow's architecture is based on a graph computation concept, where nodes represent operations (such as addition, multiplication, or convolution) and edges represent data flows (tensors).

Main Components of TensorFlow:

1. **Tensors**: These are the fundamental elements of TensorFlow. A tensor is a multi-dimensional data structure that represents arrays of data. It can have any number of dimensions, making it versatile for various machine learning applications, such as image processing or time series analysis.

2. **Computational Graphs**: Each program in TensorFlow can be represented as a computational graph. This graph describes all operations and relationships between tensors. A significant advantage of this approach is that TensorFlow can optimize the execution of the graph, distributing computations across multiple devices (such as CPUs, GPUs, or

TPUs).

3. **Sessions**: A session in TensorFlow is the environment in which the computational graph is executed. Sessions handle variable initialization and coordinate the execution of operations within the graph.

4. **Variables**: Variables are one of the fundamental elements for training models in TensorFlow. They allow for maintaining and updating the model's weights during the learning process.

5. **Eager Execution**: Starting from TensorFlow 2.0, eager execution (immediate execution) has become the default way of working. Eager execution allows operations to be performed immediately, without the need to first define a computational graph, making development and debugging much simpler and more intuitive.

6. **Multi-Platform Distribution**: TensorFlow is designed to run on different platforms, such as CPUs, GPUs, and TPUs (Tensor Processing Units, specialized processors developed by Google to accelerate machine learning). This allows operations to be scaled across server clusters, significantly improving performance for large models.

Applications of TensorFlow

TensorFlow is extremely versatile and is used in a wide range of applications:

1. **Computer Vision**: TensorFlow is used in many computer vision applications, such as object recognition, face detection, image segmentation, and visual anomaly detection. For example, convolutional neural networks (CNNs) are widely used with TensorFlow for these applications.

2. **Natural Language Processing (NLP)**:

TensorFlow is a popular choice for developing NLP models such as machine translation systems, chatbots, and text completion models. TensorFlow has supported the creation of Transformer models, such as BERT (Bidirectional Encoder Representations from Transformers) and GPT.

3. **Speech Recognition**: TensorFlow is used in speech recognition, a field that requires deep learning models capable of interpreting audio and converting it into text. Recurrent neural networks (RNNs) and Long Short-Term Memory (LSTM) networks are among the architectures used.

4. **Robotics and Control**: TensorFlow is employed in robotics for building models that enable robots to learn and adapt to their surroundings.

5. **Time Series Forecasting**: TensorFlow can be used to build models capable of predicting future events based on historical

data, such as in financial forecasting or climate analysis.

Installation and Setup

Installing TensorFlow depends on the platform and environment in which it will be used. While TensorFlow can run on a wide range of systems, there are some basic requirements that must be met to ensure proper functioning.

System Requirements

Before installing TensorFlow, it is essential to verify that the system meets some minimum requirements. The basic requirements are as follows:

- **Operating System**: TensorFlow can run on Windows, macOS, and Linux.

- **Python Version**: TensorFlow supports Python 3.7 or later versions.

- **CPU or GPU**: TensorFlow can run on CPUs, but for optimal performance (especially when training complex models), it is recommended to use a compatible GPU. Specifically, if you want to run TensorFlow on a GPU, an NVIDIA graphics card with CUDA support is required.

- **RAM**: It is recommended to have at least 8 GB of RAM, although more memory may be needed for more complex models.

GPU Usage Requirements

- **CUDA**: If you intend to use TensorFlow with an NVIDIA GPU, you need to install CUDA, a parallel computing platform developed by NVIDIA.

- **cuDNN**: NVIDIA cuDNN is a library that provides acceleration for deep learning operations on GPUs. It must be installed to take advantage of TensorFlow with GPU.

Installing TensorFlow on Different Platforms

Installation on Windows

To install TensorFlow on Windows, it is recommended to use a virtual development environment such as Anaconda, which simplifies managing dependencies and required libraries.

1. **Install Anaconda**: Download and install Anaconda from the official website. After installation, open Anaconda Prompt.

2. **Create a Virtual Environment**:

    ```bash
    conda create -n tensorflow_env python=3.8
    conda activate tensorflow_env
    ```

3. **Install TensorFlow**:

For CPU:

```bash
pip install tensorflow
```

For GPU:

```bash
pip install tensorflow-gpu
```

4. **Verify Installation**:

```bash
python -c "import tensorflow as tf; print(tf.reduce_sum(tf.random.normal([1000, 1000])))"
```

Installation on Mac

On macOS, TensorFlow can be installed with

pip within a virtual environment.

1. **Install Python 3 and pip**: Ensure that Python 3 and pip are installed. Python can be installed via Homebrew:

   ```bash
   brew install python
   ```

2. **Create a Virtual Environment**:

   ```bash
   python3 -m venv tensorflow_env
   source tensorflow_env/bin/activate
   ```

3. **Install TensorFlow**:

   ```bash
   pip install tensorflow
   ```

4. **Verify Installation**:

   ```bash
   python -c "import tensorflow as tf; print(tf.reduce_sum(tf.random.normal([1000, 1000])))"
   ```

Installation on Linux

On Linux, the installation of TensorFlow follows a process similar to Windows and macOS.

1. **Update System Packages**:

   ```bash
   sudo apt update
   sudo apt install python3-dev python3-pip
   ```

2. **Create a Virtual Environment**:

   ```bash
   python3 -m venv tensorflow_env
   source tensorflow_env/bin/activate
   ```

3. **Install TensorFlow**:

   ```bash
   pip install tensorflow
   ```

4. **Verify Installation**:

   ```bash
   python -c "import tensorflow as tf; print(tf.reduce_sum(tf.random.normal([1000, 1000])))"
   ```

Setting Up the Development Environment

Once TensorFlow is installed, it's important to correctly configure the development environment to ensure a smooth experience.

Getting Started with TensorFlow

Once TensorFlow is installed and your environment is properly configured, you're ready to start building and running machine learning models. Below is a basic workflow for creating a model in TensorFlow, which can be applied across various machine learning tasks.

Basic TensorFlow Workflow

1. **Import Libraries**: The first step in any TensorFlow project is to import the necessary libraries.

```python
import tensorflow as tf
```


2. **Load and Preprocess Data**: TensorFlow supports a variety of data types. For example, you can load datasets from TensorFlow Datasets (`tfds`) or NumPy arrays. The preprocessing stage includes normalization, data augmentation, and splitting the dataset into training and test sets.

Example: Loading the MNIST dataset (handwritten digits dataset):

```python
mnist = tf.keras.datasets.mnist
(x_train, y_train), (x_test, y_test) = mnist.load_data()
x_train, x_test = x_train / 255.0, x_test / 255.0  # Normalize pixel values
```

3. **Define the Model**: Using TensorFlow's `tf.keras` API, you can create various types of machine learning models such as Sequential models or functional API models. Sequential models are simple to use and are composed of layers stacked on top of each other.

Example: Building a simple neural network for MNIST:

```python
model = tf.keras.models.Sequential([
    tf.keras.layers.Flatten(input_shape=(28, 28)),  # Flatten input images
    tf.keras.layers.Dense(128, activation='relu'),  # Hidden layer
    tf.keras.layers.Dropout(0.2),                   # Dropout layer for regularization
    tf.keras.layers.Dense(10)                       # Output layer for 10 classes
])
```

```

4. **Compile the Model**: After defining the model architecture, it needs to be compiled by specifying the optimizer, loss function, and metrics to track during training.

Example:

```python
model.compile(optimizer='adam',

loss=tf.keras.losses.SparseCategoricalCrossentropy(from_logits=True),

        metrics=['accuracy'])
```

5. **Train the Model**: Training is the process where the model learns from the data by minimizing the loss function. During training, TensorFlow adjusts the model's weights to improve predictions.
```

Example:

```python
model.fit(x_train, y_train, epochs=5)  # Train for 5 epochs
```

6. **Evaluate the Model**: Once the model is trained, you should evaluate its performance on a test dataset to check how well it generalizes to new data.

Example:

```python
model.evaluate(x_test, y_test, verbose=2)
```

7. **Make Predictions**: After training and evaluation, you can use the model to make predictions on new data.

Example:

```python
predictions = model.predict(x_test)
```

Example of a Complete Workflow

Here's an example of a complete workflow using TensorFlow to build, train, and evaluate a basic neural network on the MNIST dataset:

```python
import tensorflow as tf

# Load and preprocess data
mnist = tf.keras.datasets.mnist
(x_train, y_train), (x_test, y_test) = mnist.load_data()
x_train, x_test = x_train / 255.0, x_test / 255.0
```

Normalize

Define the model

```python
model = tf.keras.models.Sequential([
    tf.keras.layers.Flatten(input_shape=(28, 28)),
    tf.keras.layers.Dense(128, activation='relu'),
    tf.keras.layers.Dropout(0.2),
    tf.keras.layers.Dense(10)
])
```

Compile the model

```python
model.compile(optimizer='adam',
    loss=tf.keras.losses.SparseCategoricalCrossentropy(from_logits=True),
              metrics=['accuracy'])
```

Train the model

```
model.fit(x_train, y_train, epochs=5)

# Evaluate the model
model.evaluate(x_test, y_test, verbose=2)

# Make predictions
predictions = model.predict(x_test)
```

Advanced Features in TensorFlow

Once you're comfortable with the basics, TensorFlow offers more advanced features and techniques to enhance the power and efficiency of your machine learning models.

1. **Custom Layers and Models**

You can create custom layers by subclassing

the `tf.keras.layers.Layer` class. This is useful for building complex, reusable components like attention mechanisms or novel neural network layers.

Example of a custom layer:

```python
class MyCustomLayer(tf.keras.layers.Layer):
    def __init__(self, units=32):
        super(MyCustomLayer, self).__init__()
        self.units = units

    def build(self, input_shape):
        self.w = self.add_weight(shape=(input_shape[-1], self.units),
                                 initializer='random_normal',
                                 trainable=True)
        self.b =
```

```
    self.add_weight(shape=(self.units,), initializer='zeros', trainable=True)

    def call(self, inputs):
        return tf.matmul(inputs, self.w) + self.b

# Using the custom layer in a model
model = tf.keras.models.Sequential([
    tf.keras.layers.Flatten(input_shape=(28, 28)),
    MyCustomLayer(128),
    tf.keras.layers.Dense(10)
])
```

2. **Transfer Learning**

Transfer learning is a powerful technique where you take a pre-trained model (like

VGG16, ResNet, or Inception) and fine-tune it on your own dataset. This is particularly useful when you have a limited amount of data.

Example:

```python
base_model = tf.keras.applications.MobileNetV2(input_shape=(224, 224, 3),

include_top=False,

weights='imagenet')

base_model.trainable = False  # Freeze the base model

model = tf.keras.Sequential([
    base_model,
    tf.keras.layers.GlobalAveragePooling2D(),
```

```
    tf.keras.layers.Dense(10, activation='softmax')
])

# Compile and train the model as usual
model.compile(optimizer='adam',
              loss='sparse_categorical_crossentropy',
              metrics=['accuracy'])
```

3. **Distributed Training**

TensorFlow supports distributed training, allowing you to scale up your models across multiple GPUs, TPUs, or even across different machines in a cluster. This is managed through `tf.distribute.Strategy`, with `MirroredStrategy` being one of the most commonly used strategies for multi-GPU training.

Example:

```python
strategy = tf.distribute.MirroredStrategy()

with strategy.scope():
    model = tf.keras.models.Sequential([
        tf.keras.layers.Dense(128, activation='relu', input_shape=(784,)),
        tf.keras.layers.Dense(10, activation='softmax')
    ])
    model.compile(optimizer='adam',
                  loss='sparse_categorical_crossentropy',
                  metrics=['accuracy'])

model.fit(x_train, y_train, epochs=5)
```

4. **TensorFlow Extended (TFX)**

TFX is an end-to-end platform for deploying production machine learning pipelines. It includes components for data ingestion, validation, model training, evaluation, and deployment. TFX is designed to automate and scale machine learning workflows in production environments.

5. **TensorFlow Lite**

TensorFlow Lite is a lightweight version of TensorFlow designed for mobile and embedded devices. It enables on-device machine learning by optimizing model performance for low-latency inference and smaller model sizes.

6. **TensorFlow.js**

TensorFlow.js allows you to run machine learning models directly in the browser using JavaScript. You can either train new models or run pre-trained models for tasks such as real-time object detection, image classification, and more.

TensorFlow is a powerful and versatile framework for machine learning and deep learning, suitable for projects ranging from simple models to large-scale, complex applications. By mastering the basic workflow, leveraging advanced features like custom layers and distributed training, and exploring additional tools such as TFX and TensorFlow Lite, you can build and deploy state-of-the-art machine learning models across a wide range of environments.

Whether you're just starting with TensorFlow or looking to deepen your expertise, the flexibility and scalability of the framework make it an excellent choice for a wide range of AI and machine learning projects.

2. Fundamentals of Machine Learning in TensorFlow

Machine Learning (ML) is a branch of artificial intelligence focused on developing algorithms that enable computers to learn from data without being explicitly programmed for each task. Essentially, a machine learning model is a program that improves its performance over time as it is exposed to more data.

Definition of Machine Learning

Machine Learning can be defined as the ability of a system to automatically improve its performance on a specific task by gaining experience from data processing. This process involves three key elements:

1. **Data**: The data on which the model is trained and interacts.

2. **Models**: A mathematical representation that learns patterns from the data.

3. **Algorithms**: The algorithms that optimize the model to reduce error and improve prediction accuracy.

The goal of machine learning is to create models capable of making accurate predictions on unseen data based on what they learned from training data. TensorFlow is one of the most widely used frameworks for creating and training machine learning models due to its ability to handle large data volumes and support distributed computations on CPUs, GPUs, and TPUs.

Machine Learning Pipeline

A typical machine learning pipeline follows several stages:

1. **Data collection**: Data can come from various sources like databases, sensors, or files. Raw data needs to be collected and made available for processing.

2. **Data pre-processing**: Before training the model, the data must be cleaned and transformed. This includes handling missing values, normalizing features, and labeling.

3. **Data splitting**: The dataset is divided into three parts: a training set, a validation set, and a test set. This division allows the model to generalize better to unseen data.

4. **Model selection**: The type of model to be trained depends on the problem (regression, classification, clustering, etc.).

5. **Model training**: During training, the model learns from the data and adjusts its parameters to reduce error.

6. **Model evaluation**: Once trained, the model is evaluated using the test set to measure its accuracy, precision, or other parameters.

7. **Model deployment**: The final model can be deployed into production environments to make real-time predictions or for other applications.

TensorFlow provides tools to manage all these phases of the machine learning pipeline, making it ideal for both research projects and industrial applications.

Types of Machine Learning Algorithms

Machine learning algorithms can be divided into three main categories: supervised learning, unsupervised learning, and reinforcement learning. Each of these categories is suited to different types of problems.

Supervised Learning

Supervised learning is the most common type of machine learning and involves training the model on labeled data. Each example in the dataset is associated with a correct label. The model's goal is to learn the relationship between the input data and the labels so it can predict the correct label for new, unlabeled data.

Example: Classification with TensorFlow

A common example of supervised learning is classification, where the goal is to assign a label to an input example. A classic case is the classification of images in the famous MNIST dataset, which contains images of handwritten digits. The objective is to correctly classify the images into the corresponding numbers (from 0 to 9).

An example of TensorFlow code for classification using a simple neural network:

```python
```

```python
import tensorflow as tf
from tensorflow.keras import layers, models

# Loading the MNIST dataset
mnist = tf.keras.datasets.mnist
(x_train, y_train), (x_test, y_test) = mnist.load_data()

# Normalizing the data
x_train, x_test = x_train / 255.0, x_test / 255.0

# Creating a neural network model
model = models.Sequential([
    layers.Flatten(input_shape=(28, 28)),
    layers.Dense(128, activation='relu'),
    layers.Dense(10, activation='softmax')
])
```

```python
# Compiling the model
model.compile(optimizer='adam',
              loss='sparse_categorical_crossentropy',
              metrics=['accuracy'])

# Training the model
model.fit(x_train, y_train, epochs=5)

# Evaluating the model
model.evaluate(x_test, y_test)
```

In this example, the model is trained on images of handwritten digits. The model uses the **sparse_categorical_crossentropy** loss function to measure error and the **Adam** optimization algorithm to minimize it. After training, the model can be used to predict the digits in new images.

Regression

In regression, the goal is to predict a continuous numerical value. For example, predicting house prices based on factors like size, location, and year of construction.

Example of linear regression in TensorFlow:

```python
import tensorflow as tf
import numpy as np

# Synthetic data
X = np.array([1, 2, 3, 4, 5], dtype=np.float32)
Y = np.array([1, 2, 3, 4, 5], dtype=np.float32)

# Linear regression model
model =
```

```
tf.keras.Sequential([tf.keras.layers.Dense(1, input_shape=[1])])


# Compiling the model
model.compile(optimizer='sgd', loss='mean_squared_error')


# Training the model
model.fit(X, Y, epochs=500)


# Prediction
print(model.predict([6.0]))
```
```

In this example, the model learns a simple linear relationship between X and Y, where the input and output are identical. The model can be used to make predictions for unseen input values.
```

Unsupervised Learning

Unsupervised learning does not use labeled data. The model's goal is to find patterns or structures in the data without being provided explicit answers.

Clustering

One of the most well-known unsupervised learning algorithms is clustering, which groups data into sets, or "clusters," so that items within the same cluster are more similar to each other than those in different clusters.

A common example is the **K-means** algorithm, which attempts to partition a dataset into k groups. A clustering example with TensorFlow can be implemented as follows:

```python
import tensorflow as tf
```

```python
from sklearn.cluster import KMeans
import numpy as np

# Synthetic data
X = np.array([[1, 2], [1, 4], [1, 0],
              [10, 2], [10, 4], [10, 0]])

# Perform clustering with KMeans
kmeans = KMeans(n_clusters=2)
kmeans.fit(X)

# Predicted labels (cluster to which each point belongs)
print(kmeans.labels_)
```

Dimensionality Reduction

Another application of unsupervised learning is **dimensionality reduction**, where the goal is to reduce the number of variables in the dataset without losing important information. A common algorithm for dimensionality reduction is **Principal Component Analysis (PCA)**.

Reinforcement Learning

Reinforcement learning (RL) is a technique that differs from both supervised and unsupervised learning. In RL, an agent makes decisions by interacting with an environment. The agent receives a reward or penalty for each action taken, and the goal is to maximize the total reward over time.

One of the most well-known RL algorithms is **Q-Learning**, which allows an agent to learn the optimal policy to follow in order to maximize rewards. TensorFlow can be used to implement reinforcement learning models, especially with the help of deep neural networks.

Basics of Deep Learning

Deep Learning is a subcategory of machine learning that relies on models with multiple layers of data transformation, commonly known as **deep neural networks (DNNs)**. The term "deep" refers to the number of layers in the network. Deep neural networks are particularly effective at learning complex representations from data, such as images, text, or sound.

Artificial Neural Networks (ANN)

An **artificial neural network** is composed of nodes (or neurons) organized in layers. Each node in a layer receives input from the nodes in the previous layer, applies an activation function, and sends the result to the next layer.

The layers of a neural network generally come in three types:

1. **Input layer**: Receives raw data.

2. **Hidden layer**: Applies transformations to the data.

3. **Output layer**: Returns the final prediction.

Example of a simple neural network in TensorFlow:

```python
import tensorflow as tf
from tensorflow.keras import layers

# Defining a simple neural network
model = tf.keras.Sequential([
    layers.Dense(128, activation='relu', input_shape=(784,)),
    layers.Dense(10, activation='softmax')
])
```

Compiling the model

```
model.compile(optimizer='adam', loss='sparse_categorical_crossentropy', metrics=['accuracy'])
```

Activation Functions

Activation functions are essential for introducing non-linearity in neural networks. The most common include:

- **ReLU (Rectified Linear Unit)**: Activates only positive values, deactivating negative ones.

- **Sigmoid**: Limits values between 0 and 1, often used for binary classification problems.

- **Softmax**: Converts a vector of real values into probabilities, typically used in the output layer for multi-class classification problems.

Neural Network Training

Training a neural network involves using optimization algorithms like **Adam** or **SGD** to minimize a loss function, such as **mean squared error** or **cross-entropy**. Training proceeds in **epochs**, during which the model sees the entire dataset one or more times.

Backpropagation and Gradient Descent

During training, a process called **backpropagation** is used to update the weights of the network. Backpropagation leverages the **gradient descent** algorithm, which calculates the gradient of the loss function with respect to the model's weights and iteratively updates them to minimize the loss.

Example of Convolutional Neural Network (CNN)

Convolutional neural networks (CNNs) are commonly used for tasks like image classification because they can efficiently learn spatial hierarchies of features from input images.

```python
import tensorflow as tf
from tensorflow.keras import layers, models

# Define a simple CNN model
model = models.Sequential([
    layers.Conv2D(32, (3, 3), activation='relu', input_shape=(28, 28, 1)),
    layers.MaxPooling2D((2, 2)),
    layers.Conv2D(64, (3, 3), activation='relu'),
    layers.MaxPooling2D((2, 2)),
```

```
    layers.Flatten(),
    layers.Dense(64, activation='relu'),
    layers.Dense(10, activation='softmax')
])


# Compile the model
model.compile(optimizer='adam',
loss='sparse_categorical_crossentropy',
metrics=['accuracy'])
```

In this example, the CNN contains convolutional layers followed by pooling layers. These layers extract features from the input images and learn to classify them.

TensorFlow allows for flexible and powerful implementation of a wide range of machine learning algorithms. Its capability to scale and work on various hardware setups makes it suitable for everything from small personal projects to industrial-scale machine learning applications.

3. Data Structures in TensorFlow

The fundamental data structure used in TensorFlow is the **Tensor**, a multidimensional array representing data. Tensors are similar to vectors or matrices used in linear algebra, but they can extend to higher dimensions.

In this guide, we will explore the main data structures in TensorFlow, how they work, and how they can be used to solve complex numerical computation and machine learning problems.

Topics Covered

- What are **Tensors** in TensorFlow

- **Operations on Tensors**: mathematical operations and manipulation

- **Eager Execution**: dynamic tensor execution

- **Computation Graphs**: automatic

differentiation with computational graphs

Tensors: The Fundamental Data Structure

A **Tensor** is a multidimensional array that can contain scalars, vectors, matrices, or more complex data structures. Tensors generalize these structures to n dimensions. Every tensor has three main attributes:

1. **Rank**: The number of dimensions of the tensor. A rank-0 tensor is a scalar, a rank-1 tensor is a vector, and so on.

2. **Shape**: The number of elements in each dimension. For example, a 2x3 tensor has a shape of `(2, 3)`.

3. **Data type (dtype)**: The data type of the elements in the tensor (e.g., `float32`, `int32`, `bool`).

In TensorFlow, tensors are immutable, meaning once created, their values cannot be changed. To modify a tensor, you need to create a new one. Tensors can be created from NumPy arrays, Python lists, or directly using TensorFlow functions.

Creating a Tensor

In TensorFlow, a tensor can be created in various ways. One of the most common methods is using the `tf.constant` function, which creates an immutable tensor.

```python
import tensorflow as tf

# Create a constant tensor (rank 0: scalar)
scalar_tensor = tf.constant(42)
print("Scalar Tensor:", scalar_tensor)

# Create a rank-1 tensor (vector)
```

```
vector_tensor = tf.constant([1.0, 2.0, 3.0])
print("Vector Tensor:", vector_tensor)

# Create a rank-2 tensor (matrix)
matrix_tensor = tf.constant([[1, 2], [3, 4], [5, 6]])
print("Matrix Tensor:", matrix_tensor)

# Higher rank tensor (3x3x2)
tensor_3d = tf.constant([[[1, 2], [3, 4], [5, 6]],
            [[7, 8], [9, 10], [11, 12]],
            [[13, 14], [15, 16], [17, 18]]])
print("3D Tensor:", tensor_3d)
```

Tensor Properties

Each tensor in TensorFlow has several important properties:

- **Rank**: The number of dimensions of the tensor.

- **Shape**: The number of elements per dimension.

- **Data type (Dtype)**: The type of data it contains.

For example, we can access these properties with the following methods:

```python
# Print tensor properties
print("Shape:", tensor_3d.shape)
print("Rank:", tf.rank(tensor_3d))
print("Dtype:", tensor_3d.dtype)
```

Special Tensors

TensorFlow provides several predefined functions to create special tensors, such as tensors filled with zeros, ones, or random values:

```python
# Tensor filled with zeros
zero_tensor = tf.zeros([3, 3])
print("Zero Tensor:", zero_tensor)

# Tensor filled with ones
ones_tensor = tf.ones([2, 2])
print("Ones Tensor:", ones_tensor)

# Random value tensor
random_tensor = tf.random.uniform([2, 2], minval=0, maxval=10)
print("Random Tensor:", random_tensor)
```

Operations on Tensors

Tensors in TensorFlow support a wide range of mathematical operations, from basic algebraic operations to more complex transformations. Operations on tensors can be performed element-wise or using broadcasting, similar to NumPy arrays.

Basic Mathematical Operations

TensorFlow includes functions to perform basic mathematical operations like addition, subtraction, multiplication, and division:

```python
# Addition of two tensors
tensor_a = tf.constant([1, 2, 3])
tensor_b = tf.constant([4, 5, 6])
sum_tensor = tf.add(tensor_a, tensor_b)
```

```
print("Sum:", sum_tensor)

# Subtraction
sub_tensor = tf.subtract(tensor_a, tensor_b)
print("Subtraction:", sub_tensor)

# Multiplication
mul_tensor = tf.multiply(tensor_a, tensor_b)
print("Multiplication:", mul_tensor)

# Division
div_tensor = tf.divide(tensor_a, tensor_b)
print("Division:", div_tensor)
```

Broadcasting

Broadcasting is a technique used by

TensorFlow (similar to NumPy) to perform operations on tensors of different sizes. If the tensor shapes do not match exactly, TensorFlow will attempt to match the smaller dimensions to the larger ones.

```python
tensor_c = tf.constant([[1, 2], [3, 4], [5, 6]])
tensor_d = tf.constant([1, 2])

# Broadcasting allows the vector to be "extended" to match the shape of the tensor
result = tf.add(tensor_c, tensor_d)
print("Broadcasting Result:", result)
```

Reduction Operations

Reduction operations are used to compute aggregated values over specific dimensions of a tensor. Some common reduction operations include sum, mean, and max:

```python
# 2D Tensor
matrix_tensor = tf.constant([[1, 2], [3, 4], [5, 6]])

# Sum across all dimensions
total_sum = tf.reduce_sum(matrix_tensor)
print("Total Sum:", total_sum)

# Sum by column (axis 0)
col_sum = tf.reduce_sum(matrix_tensor, axis=0)
print("Column Sum:", col_sum)

# Sum by row (axis 1)
row_sum = tf.reduce_sum(matrix_tensor,
```

```
axis=1)
print("Row Sum:", row_sum)

# Max value
max_value = tf.reduce_max(matrix_tensor)
print("Max Value:", max_value)
```

Tensor Transformations

It is also possible to transform tensors into different shapes or change their data types:

```python
# Reshape a tensor
reshaped_tensor = tf.reshape(matrix_tensor, [2, 3])
print("Reshaped Tensor:", reshaped_tensor)
```

```
# Change tensor data type
float_tensor = tf.cast(matrix_tensor, dtype=tf.float32)
print("Converted Tensor to float:", float_tensor)
```

Eager Execution

One of the most significant approaches introduced in TensorFlow is **Eager Execution**, which allows for immediate execution of operations without the need to build an explicit computational graph. In eager mode, tensor operations are executed immediately, returning concrete results instead of symbolic objects. This makes TensorFlow more intuitive and easier to use for debugging and prototyping.

Enabling Eager Execution

By default, TensorFlow 2.0 and later automatically enable Eager Execution, so manual activation is unnecessary. However, in earlier versions of TensorFlow, it had to be explicitly enabled:

```python
import tensorflow as tf

# Enable Eager Execution (only needed for TensorFlow 1.x)
tf.config.run_functions_eagerly(True)

# Operations in eager mode
tensor_x = tf.constant([1.0, 2.0, 3.0])
tensor_y = tf.constant([4.0, 5.0, 6.0])

result = tf.add(tensor_x, tensor_y)
print("Result with Eager Execution:", result)
```

In eager mode, you can immediately view the results of operations without constructing a computation graph:

```python
print("Sum:", result.numpy())  # Convert a tensor to a NumPy array
```

Benefits of Eager Execution

Eager Execution offers several advantages, including:

- **Ease of debugging**: With immediate execution, it's easier to catch errors during development.

- **Interoperability with NumPy**: Tensors can be easily converted to NumPy arrays and vice versa, enhancing integration with Python libraries.

- **Python-like experience**: Eager Execution makes TensorFlow feel more like a typical programming library, without the complexity of graph construction.

However, Eager Execution may not be optimal for large-scale production scenarios, where a static computation graph remains more efficient.

Computation Graphs

In traditional TensorFlow mode (pre-2.0), tensor operations are not executed immediately but are represented as a **computation graph**. This graph is a symbolic representation of operations and data flows, which can be optimized and executed later.

Advantages of Computation Graphs

Using computation graphs offers several key benefits:

- **Efficiency**: Graphs enable the optimization of operations to minimize memory consumption and speed up computation.

- **Portability**: A computation graph can be saved and loaded on different machines, allowing execution on heterogeneous platforms like CPU, GPU, or TPU.

- **Distribution**: Graphs can be distributed across multiple devices, facilitating large-scale training.

Creating and Executing a Computation Graph

Although Eager Execution is enabled by default in TensorFlow 2.x, it is still possible to use computation graphs for their efficiency. To do this, you need to define a function representing the graph:


```python
import tensorflow as tf
```

```python
# Define a function that creates a computation graph
@tf.function
def graph_function(x, y):
    return tf.add(x, y)

# Use the computation graph
tensor_x = tf.constant([1.0, 2.0, 3.0])
tensor_y = tf.constant([4.0, 5.0, 6.0])

# This runs within a computation graph context
result_graph = graph_function(tensor_x, tensor_y)
print("Result from Computation Graph:", result_graph)
```

When using the `@tf.function` decorator, TensorFlow automatically converts the function into a static computation graph for performance optimization.

Automatic Differentiation

TensorFlow's computation graphs also support **automatic differentiation**, which is essential for deep learning. TensorFlow can automatically compute gradients of functions with respect to their inputs, which is useful for optimizing models during training.

To compute gradients, you can use the `tf.GradientTape` context manager:

```python
# Define a function with trainable variables
def compute_loss(x, y):
    w = tf.Variable([1.0, 2.0, 3.0])
```

```python
    return tf.reduce_mean(tf.square(tf.multiply(x, w) - y))

# Compute gradients with respect to variables
x = tf.constant([1.0, 2.0, 3.0])
y = tf.constant([3.0, 6.0, 9.0])

with tf.GradientTape() as tape:
    loss = compute_loss(x, y)

gradients = tape.gradient(loss, [w])
print("Gradients:", gradients)
```
```

TensorFlow's data structures and operations are at the core of its ability to handle complex numerical computations. With eager execution, it becomes more intuitive to write and debug code, while computation graphs
```

provide the efficiency and scalability necessary for production-grade deep learning systems. Understanding how to manipulate tensors, perform operations on them, and leverage computation graphs is crucial for harnessing TensorFlow's full power.

4. Model Building in TensorFlow

Building models in TensorFlow is one of the core skills for anyone looking to utilize this powerful library for deep learning. TensorFlow provides tools to create, train, evaluate, and optimize complex models. In this document, we will explore various approaches to model building, including sequential models, functional models, and custom models. We will then look at how to train and evaluate models and discuss the importance of neural networks, as well as optimization and regularization techniques.

Model Building in TensorFlow

1. Sequential Models

The **sequential model** is one of the simplest to implement in TensorFlow using the Keras API. A sequential model is a linear stack of layers, where the output of each layer becomes the input of the next.

Creating a Sequential Model

Let's see how to build a sequential model that includes multiple dense layers:

```python
import tensorflow as tf
from tensorflow.keras import layers

# Define a sequential model
model = tf.keras.Sequential([
    layers.Dense(64, activation='relu', input_shape=(100,)),  # First layer
    layers.Dense(64, activation='relu'),  # Second layer
    layers.Dense(10, activation='softmax')  # Output layer
```

```
])

# Compile the model
model.compile(optimizer='adam',
loss='sparse_categorical_crossentropy',
metrics=['accuracy'])

# Print the model summary
model.summary()
```

In this example, the model has two dense (fully connected) layers with 64 neurons each, and an output layer with 10 neurons, suitable for a multi-class classification problem.

2. Functional Models

Unlike the sequential model, the **functional model** in TensorFlow allows you to create more complex neural networks, such as those with layers that receive multiple inputs or produce multiple outputs.

Creating a Functional Model

Here's an example of building a functional model:

```python
from tensorflow.keras import Input, Model

# Define the input
inputs = Input(shape=(784,))

# Define the data flow
x = layers.Dense(64, activation='relu')(inputs)
x = layers.Dense(64, activation='relu')(x)
outputs = layers.Dense(10,
```

```python
activation='softmax')(x)

# Create the functional model
model = Model(inputs=inputs, outputs=outputs)

# Compile the model
model.compile(optimizer='adam',
loss='sparse_categorical_crossentropy',
metrics=['accuracy'])

# Print the model summary
model.summary()
```
```

This approach is more flexible than the sequential model, as it allows you to connect arbitrary layers, enabling the creation of complex network architectures.
```

3. Custom Models

TensorFlow also allows you to create fully custom models using the `tf.keras.Model` subclass. This approach is useful when you need to implement non-standard neural network architectures or incorporate custom operations.

Creating a Custom Model

Here's an example of building a custom model:

```python
class MyModel(tf.keras.Model):
    def __init__(self):
        super(MyModel, self).__init__()
        self.dense1 = layers.Dense(64, activation='relu')
```

```python
        self.dense2 = layers.Dense(10, activation='softmax')

    def call(self, inputs):
        x = self.dense1(inputs)
        return self.dense2(x)

# Create an instance of the custom model
model = MyModel()

# Compile the model
model.compile(optimizer='adam', loss='sparse_categorical_crossentropy', metrics=['accuracy'])

# Print the model summary
model.build(input_shape=(None, 784))
model.summary()
```

This approach offers maximum flexibility, allowing you to fully customize the model's behavior.

4. Training a Model

Once the model is built, you can train it using the `fit()` method. During training, the model learns from the provided data and updates its weights iteratively.

```python
# Create some sample data
import numpy as np
x_train = np.random.random((1000, 784))
y_train = np.random.randint(10, size=(1000,))

# Train the model
model.fit(x_train, y_train, epochs=10, batch_size=32)
```

```

### 5. Evaluating a Model

After training, you can evaluate the model's performance on test data using the `evaluate()` method:

```python
# Create test data
x_test = np.random.random((100, 784))
y_test = np.random.randint(10, size=(100,))

# Evaluate the model
loss, accuracy = model.evaluate(x_test, y_test)
print(f"Test Loss: {loss}, Test Accuracy: {accuracy}")
```
```

Neural Networks in TensorFlow

1. Artificial Neural Networks (ANN)

Artificial Neural Networks (ANN) are the foundation of many deep learning models. An ANN consists of layers of artificial neurons that process and transform the input. Each neuron performs a linear combination of the input followed by a non-linear activation function.

Here's an example of a simple ANN:

```python
model = tf.keras.Sequential([
    layers.Dense(128, activation='relu', input_shape=(784,)),
    layers.Dense(64, activation='relu'),
    layers.Dense(10, activation='softmax')
```

])
```

### 2. Convolutional Neural Networks (CNN)

**Convolutional Neural Networks** (CNN) are designed to process grid-like structured data, such as images. They use convolutional layers to extract features from the input data, followed by pooling layers to reduce dimensionality.

Here's an example of a CNN for image classification:

```python
model = tf.keras.Sequential([
    layers.Conv2D(32, (3, 3), activation='relu', input_shape=(28, 28, 1)),
    layers.MaxPooling2D((2, 2)),

```python
    layers.Conv2D(64, (3, 3), activation='relu'),
    layers.MaxPooling2D((2, 2)),
    layers.Flatten(),
    layers.Dense(64, activation='relu'),
    layers.Dense(10, activation='softmax')
])
```

3. Recurrent Neural Networks (RNN)

Recurrent Neural Networks (RNN) are used to process sequential data, such as text or time series. RNNs maintain a memory of previous steps, allowing them to process data sequences.

```python
model = tf.keras.Sequential([
    layers.SimpleRNN(64, input_shape=(100, 10), return_sequences=True),
```

```
    layers.SimpleRNN(64),
    layers.Dense(10, activation='softmax')
])
```

4. Advanced Architectures (LSTM, GRU, etc.)

LSTMs (Long Short-Term Memory) and **GRUs** (Gated Recurrent Units) are variants of RNNs designed to overcome long-term memory issues in standard RNNs.

Example of LSTM:

```python
model = tf.keras.Sequential([
    layers.LSTM(64, input_shape=(100, 10)),
    layers.Dense(10, activation='softmax')
```

])
```

#### Example of GRU:

```python
model = tf.keras.Sequential([
    layers.GRU(64, input_shape=(100, 10)),
    layers.Dense(10, activation='softmax')
])
```

Optimization and Regularization in TensorFlow

1. Loss Functions

Loss functions are used to quantify the error of the model during training. Some
```

commonly used loss functions in TensorFlow include:

- **Mean Squared Error**: `tf.keras.losses.MeanSquaredError()`

- **Categorical Crossentropy**: `tf.keras.losses.CategoricalCrossentropy()` or `SparseCategoricalCrossentropy()` for classification problems

- **Binary Crossentropy**: For binary classification problems.

An example of using a loss function in TensorFlow:

```python
# Compile the model with a loss function and optimization algorithm
model.compile(optimizer='adam', loss=tf.keras.losses.SparseCategoricalCrossentropy(), metrics=['accuracy'])
```

2. Optimization Algorithms

Optimization algorithms are used to minimize the loss function by updating the model's weights through an iterative process. Some of the most commonly used optimization algorithms in TensorFlow include:

- **SGD** (Stochastic Gradient Descent)
- **Adam** (Adaptive Moment Estimation)
- **RMSprop**: Particularly effective for recurrent neural networks.

An example of compiling the model with the Adam algorithm:

```python
model.compile(optimizer=tf.keras.optimizers.Adam(learning_rate=0.001),
```

```
    loss='sparse_categorical_crossentropy',
    metrics=['accuracy'])
```

3. Regularization Techniques

Regularization helps prevent overfitting, which occurs when the model fits too well to the training data but does not generalize well to test data. TensorFlow offers various regularization techniques.

L2 Regularization (Ridge)

L2 regularization adds a penalty on the squared weights in the loss function, improving the model's generalization.

```python
```

```
model.add(layers.Dense(64, kernel_regularizer=tf.keras.regularizers.l2(0.01), activation='relu'))
```

Dropout

Dropout is another regularization technique where some neurons are randomly "dropped out" during training to prevent the model from overfitting.

```python
model.add(layers.Dropout(0.5))  # 50% of the neurons are dropped out
```

4. Callbacks and Early Stopping

Callbacks are tools that allow you to

monitor training and intervene to stop the process under certain conditions. One of the most useful callbacks is **Early Stopping**, which halts training when the model stops improving on validation performance.

Early Stopping

```python
early_stopping = tf.keras.callbacks.EarlyStopping(monitor='val_loss', patience=3)

# Train the model with the callback
history = model.fit(x_train, y_train, validation_data=(x_val, y_val), epochs=50, callbacks=[early_stopping])
```

In this example, training will stop if the validation loss does not improve for 3 consecutive epochs.

TensorFlow offers a wide range of tools for building, training, evaluating, and optimizing machine learning models. From sequential models to functional models and custom models, TensorFlow allows great flexibility in model architecture. Artificial neural networks, convolutional networks, and recurrent networks form the core of deep learning applications, while regularization, optimization, and callback techniques help improve the quality of trained models.

To tackle complex problems, TensorFlow also offers advanced tools for leveraging architectures such as LSTM and GRU to process sequential data, making it a comprehensive platform for large-scale deep learning applications.

5. Datasets and Preprocessing in TensorFlow

Data management and preprocessing are critical phases in the development of machine learning and deep learning models. Datasets need to be loaded, transformed, and prepared to train effective models. TensorFlow provides various tools for these tasks, including `tf.data` for efficient data manipulation and Keras for preprocessing. Moreover, techniques like data augmentation and integration with monitoring and deployment tools such as TensorBoard and TensorFlow Serving are essential for deploying models into production.

In this document, we will explore the following areas:

1. Loading and managing data

2. Preprocessing techniques

3. Custom datasets with `tf.data`

4. Data augmentation

5. Integration with other tools, like TensorBoard and TensorFlow Serving

---

1. Loading and Managing Data

The first step in building a model is loading the data. TensorFlow provides several ways to do this, especially through predefined datasets, like those available via `tensorflow_datasets` (TFDS), or by loading custom data from files like CSV, images, or relational databases.

Loading Predefined Datasets

TensorFlow offers a wide range of predefined datasets via `tensorflow_datasets`. These datasets are commonly used in research and can be easily loaded.

```python
import tensorflow as tf
import tensorflow_datasets as tfds

# Load a predefined dataset (e.g., MNIST)
(ds_train, ds_test), ds_info = tfds.load('mnist', split=['train', 'test'], shuffle_files=True, as_supervised=True, with_info=True)

# Display dataset information
print(ds_info)
```

In this example, we are loading the MNIST dataset, a dataset of handwritten digits. `as_supervised=True` means the data will be loaded as `(image, label)` pairs.

Loading Custom Datasets

If your data is stored in CSV format, TensorFlow provides utilities to load and preprocess them easily.

```python
# Load a CSV file
dataset = tf.data.experimental.make_csv_dataset(
    'data.csv',
    batch_size=32,
    label_name='label_column',
    num_epochs=1
)

# Display a batch of the dataset
for batch in dataset.take(1):
    features, labels = batch
    print(features)
```

```
    print(labels)
```

This loads a CSV dataset in batches of 32 and defines which column represents the labels (target). The remaining columns are treated as features.

2. Preprocessing Techniques

Data preprocessing is an essential step to transform raw data into a format suitable for training models. TensorFlow provides several tools and preprocessing functionalities, such as normalization, text and image processing, and handling missing data.

Image Preprocessing

For images, it's common to resize, normalize, and apply specific transformations.

```python
# Image preprocessing function
def preprocess_image(image, label):
    image = tf.image.resize(image, [28, 28])  # Resize to 28x28
    image = tf.cast(image, tf.float32) / 255.0  # Normalize pixel values between 0 and 1
    return image, label


# Apply preprocessing function to the MNIST dataset
ds_train = ds_train.map(preprocess_image, num_parallel_calls=tf.data.experimental.AUTOTUNE)
```

Text Data Preprocessing

When working with text, it is often necessary

to tokenize and convert strings into sequences of numbers. TensorFlow provides tools like `TextVectorization` to handle this conversion.

```python
from tensorflow.keras.layers import TextVectorization

# Define the tokenization layer
vectorize_layer = TextVectorization(
    max_tokens=10000,
    output_mode='int',
    output_sequence_length=100
)

# Adapt the layer to the dataset's vocabulary
vectorize_layer.adapt(train_text_data)

# Apply the layer to the data
```

```
text_vectorized =
vectorize_layer(raw_text_batch)

print(text_vectorized)
```

3. Custom Datasets with `tf.data`

`tf.data` is a powerful module in TensorFlow that allows you to create efficient and flexible data pipelines. It offers numerous operations to manipulate and transform datasets, which can be loaded in batches and optimized to speed up model training.

Creating a Dataset with `tf.data`

`tf.data.Dataset` can be used to create datasets from NumPy arrays, Python lists, or files. Here's an example of creating a dataset from NumPy arrays:

```python
import numpy as np

# Create example data
x = np.random.random((1000, 32))
y = np.random.randint(10, size=(1000, 1))

# Create a dataset from NumPy arrays
dataset = tf.data.Dataset.from_tensor_slices((x, y))

# Split the dataset into batches
dataset = dataset.batch(32)
```

Dataset Pipelines with `tf.data`

The `tf.data` pipeline can be used to transform and optimize datasets for efficient execution.

For instance, you can combine operations like mapping, shuffling, and batching to create powerful pipelines.

```python
# Complete pipeline
dataset = dataset.shuffle(1000).map(preprocess_image).batch(32).prefetch(tf.data.experimental.AUTOTUNE)
```

Handling Large Datasets

If working with large datasets that can't be loaded entirely into memory, `tf.data` can handle the data incrementally through operations like `from_generator()` or `from_tensors()`.

```python
```

```
def generator():
    for i in range(1000):
        yield (np.random.random((32,)), np.random.randint(10))

# Create a dataset from a generator
dataset = tf.data.Dataset.from_generator(generator, output_signature=(
    tf.TensorSpec(shape=(32,), dtype=tf.float32),
    tf.TensorSpec(shape=(), dtype=tf.int32))
)
```

4. Data Augmentation

Data augmentation is a technique used to increase the diversity of an existing dataset by applying random transformations, such as rotations, zoom, or translations to images. TensorFlow offers built-in functions for data augmentation, especially for images.

Image Augmentation with `tf.image`

```python
def augment_image(image, label):
    image = tf.image.random_flip_left_right(image)
    image = tf.image.random_brightness(image, max_delta=0.2)
    return image, label

# Apply augmentation to the dataset
ds_train = ds_train.map(augment_image, num_parallel_calls=tf.data.experimental.AUTOTUNE)
```

Augmentation with `tf.keras.preprocessing`

In addition to `tf.image`, TensorFlow also provides specific augmentation tools in the Keras API, such as `RandomFlip`, `RandomRotation`, and `RandomZoom`.

```python
from tensorflow.keras.preprocessing import image_dataset_from_directory

# Load images from a directory and apply augmentation
train_dataset = image_dataset_from_directory(
    'path_to_images',
    image_size=(256, 256),
    batch_size=32,
```

```
    shuffle=True
)


# Augmentation through Keras layers
augmentation_layer = tf.keras.Sequential([
layers.RandomFlip("horizontal_and_vertical"),
    layers.RandomRotation(0.2),
])

augmented_ds = train_dataset.map(lambda x, y: (augmentation_layer(x, training=True), y))
```

5. Integration with Other Tools

TensorFlow can be integrated with various tools that facilitate model development, monitoring, and deployment. In this section, we explore how to use TensorFlow with Keras, TensorBoard, and TensorFlow Serving.

Using TensorFlow with Keras

Keras is integrated into TensorFlow and provides a user-friendly, high-level interface to build and train deep learning models. By using Keras, we can leverage TensorFlow's high-level functionality.

```python
# Creating a model with Keras and TensorFlow
model = tf.keras.Sequential([
    layers.Dense(128, activation='relu', input_shape=(784,)),
    layers.Dropout(0.2),
    layers.Dense(10, activation='softmax')
])
```

```
model.compile(optimizer='adam',

loss='sparse_categorical_crossentropy',
        metrics=['accuracy'])

# Train the model
model.fit(x_train, y_train, epochs=5)
```

Integration with TensorBoard

TensorBoard is a visualization tool that allows real-time monitoring of model training. You can visualize metrics like loss and accuracy, analyze computation graphs, and inspect model weights.

```python
# Define the TensorBoard callback
```

```
tensorboard_callback = tf.keras.callbacks.TensorBoard(log_dir="./logs")

# Train the model with TensorBoard
model.fit(x_train, y_train, epochs=5, callbacks=[tensorboard_callback])
```

To view the logs in TensorBoard:

```bash
tensorboard --logdir ./logs
```

Using TensorFlow Serving

TensorFlow Serving is a flexible, high-performance system for serving machine learning models in production. It allows you to serve TensorFlow models via a REST or gRPC API.

```bash
# Save the model in a servable format
model.save('my_model')

# Start TensorFlow Serving
tensorflow_model_server --rest_api_port=8501 --model_name=my_model --model_base_path="/path_to_model/"
```

Deploying TensorFlow Models

Once a model is trained, it can be deployed in various environments, such as mobile devices (TensorFlow Lite) or web browsers (TensorFlow.js).

Example of converting a model for TensorFlow Lite:

```python
converter = tf.lite.TFLiteConverter.from_saved_model('my_model')
tflite_model = converter.convert()

# Save the converted model
with open('model.tflite', 'wb') as f:
    f.write(tflite_model)
```

Data processing and preprocessing are essential steps to ensure that machine learning models are accurate and efficient. TensorFlow offers a variety of tools to handle complex and custom datasets, supporting advanced techniques like data augmentation and integration with monitoring and deployment tools. With its flexibility and scalability, TensorFlow simplifies the process of training and deploying

models at scale, making it a leading platform for machine learning and deep learning.

6. TensorFlow and the Cloud

As the complexity and size of machine learning (ML) models increase, the need for high computational power and adequate storage resources has become a priority. Using the cloud to train and deploy ML models allows developers to access scalable and powerful resources without having to invest in expensive infrastructure. TensorFlow, one of the most popular machine learning libraries, integrates seamlessly with various cloud services such as Google Cloud Platform (GCP) and Amazon Web Services (AWS), and can fully leverage the machine learning as a service (MLaaS) offered by these providers.

This article explores how TensorFlow can be used in the cloud, focusing on:

- TensorFlow on Google Cloud

- Using TensorFlow on AWS

- Cloud Machine Learning Services

---

1. TensorFlow on Google Cloud

Google Cloud Platform (GCP) offers a wide range of services for running machine learning models using TensorFlow. Since TensorFlow was originally developed by Google, the integration of TensorFlow with GCP is extremely smooth, providing optimized tools and infrastructure for training and deploying models at scale.

1.1 Google AI Platform

Google AI Platform is a comprehensive machine learning service on GCP that allows for the training, evaluation, and deployment of TensorFlow models at scale. It provides scalable computing resources, support for TPU (Tensor Processing Unit) and GPU, and model lifecycle management services.

Steps to train a model on Google AI Platform:

1. **Prepare your data**: Data can be stored in Google Cloud Storage (GCS), BigQuery, or another supported storage service.

2. **Write the TensorFlow code**: Training code can be written using TensorFlow as if it were running locally, but with some specific cloud configurations, such as checkpoint management and saving models directly to Google Cloud Storage.

3. **Run the training on AI Platform**:

```bash
gcloud ai-platform jobs submit training my_job_name \
  --module-name=trainer.task \
  --package-path=./trainer \
  --region=us-central1 \
```

```
--python-version=3.8 \
--runtime-version=2.4 \
--job-dir=gs://my_bucket/my_model_dir \
--scale-tier=BASIC_GPU
```

4. **Monitor the training**: Use TensorBoard or AI Platform's native monitoring tools to observe your model's progress. You can track metrics such as loss and accuracy in real time.

Example Training Configuration

If using a saved TensorFlow model, training on AI Platform requires packaging the training code into a Python module (e.g., trainer/task.py).

```python
import tensorflow as tf
```

```python
def train_and_evaluate(output_dir):
    # Load data
    (x_train, y_train), (x_test, y_test) = tf.keras.datasets.mnist.load_data()

    # Normalize data
    x_train, x_test = x_train / 255.0, x_test / 255.0

    # Define the model
    model = tf.keras.models.Sequential([
        tf.keras.layers.Flatten(input_shape=(28, 28)),
        tf.keras.layers.Dense(128, activation='relu'),
        tf.keras.layers.Dropout(0.2),
        tf.keras.layers.Dense(10, activation='softmax')
    ])
```

```
# Compile the model
model.compile(optimizer='adam',
              loss='sparse_categorical_crossentropy',
              metrics=['accuracy'])

# Train the model
model.fit(x_train, y_train, epochs=5)

# Save the model to Google Cloud Storage
model.save(output_dir)
```

1.2 Using TPUs on Google Cloud

TPUs are specialized chips designed by Google to accelerate the training and inference of deep learning models, particularly TensorFlow. To use a TPU on GCP, you can simply select it as a computing resource when configuring a training job on AI Platform.

Training with TPU:

1. **Configure the job with gcloud**:

   ```bash
   gcloud ai-platform jobs submit training my_tpu_job \
     --module-name=trainer.task \
     --package-path=./trainer \
     --region=us-central1 \
     --python-version=3.8 \
     --runtime-version=2.4 \
     --scale-tier=BASIC_TPU
   ```

2. **Update the code for TPUs**: TensorFlow allows a smooth transition from CPU/GPU to TPU with the

`tf.distribute.TPUStrategy` API:

```python
# Define strategy for TPU training
resolver = tf.distribute.cluster_resolver.TPUClusterResolver()

tf.config.experimental_connect_to_cluster(resolver)

tf.tpu.experimental.initialize_tpu_system(resolver)
strategy = tf.distribute.TPUStrategy(resolver)

# Within the strategy, define the model and training
with strategy.scope():
    model = tf.keras.Sequential([...])
    model.compile(optimizer='adam', loss='sparse_categorical_crossentropy',
```

```
metrics=['accuracy'])
model.fit(x_train, y_train, epochs=5)
```

1.3 TensorFlow Extended (TFX) on Google Cloud

TFX is an end-to-end platform for automating the TensorFlow model lifecycle. On GCP, TFX can be run using AI Platform Pipelines, which simplifies managing and orchestrating machine learning workflows, allowing you to build modular and reusable pipelines.

Example of a TFX pipeline for GCP:

```python
import tfx
from tfx.components import CsvExampleGen, Trainer, Evaluator
from tfx.orchestration.experimental.interactive.inter
```

```python
active_context import InteractiveContext

# Define the context
context = InteractiveContext()

# Define the CsvExampleGen component for data loading
example_gen = CsvExampleGen(input_base='gs://my_bucket/data')
context.run(example_gen)

# Define the trainer with a Keras model
trainer = Trainer(module_file='trainer.py',

examples=example_gen.outputs['examples'],

train_args=tfx.proto.TrainArgs(num_steps=100),
```

```
    eval_args=tfx.proto.EvalArgs(num_steps=50)
)

context.run(trainer)
```

TFX includes components for transforming data, training models, evaluating them, and deploying scalable machine learning pipelines, all executable on GCP.

2. Using TensorFlow on AWS

Amazon Web Services (AWS) is another leading cloud provider that supports TensorFlow through various services such as Amazon SageMaker, EC2 with GPU support, and S3 for data storage.

2.1 Amazon SageMaker

Amazon SageMaker is AWS's managed

machine learning service that allows building, training, and deploying machine learning models at scale. SageMaker supports direct integration with TensorFlow, enabling model training on distributed clusters without manually managing the infrastructure.

Steps to train a TensorFlow model on SageMaker:

1. **Configure the SageMaker environment:**

```python
import sagemaker
from sagemaker.tensorflow import TensorFlow

# Define the SageMaker session and training parameters
sagemaker_session = sagemaker.Session()
role =
```

```
'arn:aws:iam::123456789012:role/SageMakerRole'

# Create a TensorFlow training job
tf_estimator = TensorFlow(entry_point='train.py',
                          role=role,
                          instance_count=1,
                          instance_type='ml.p2.xlarge',
                          framework_version='2.4.1',
                          py_version='py37')

# Start the training
tf_estimator.fit({'train': 's3://my-bucket/train-data',
                  'test': 's3://my-bucket/test-data'})
```

2. **Deploy the model on SageMaker:**

After training the model, you can deploy it for inference using SageMaker Hosting:

```python
# Deploy the model to a SageMaker endpoint
predictor = tf_estimator.deploy(initial_instance_count=1, instance_type='ml.m5.xlarge')
```

3. **Inference on SageMaker:**

Once the model is deployed, you can send inference requests:

```python
# Send data for inference
response = predictor.predict(data)
print(response)
```

2.2 Amazon EC2 with GPU Support

Amazon EC2 offers GPU instances that can be used to train TensorFlow models. These instances, such as `p3.2xlarge` and `p4d.24xlarge`, are optimized for deep learning and provide access to high computational resources.

Using EC2 for Training:

1. **Launch an EC2 instance**: Select a GPU instance from the AWS Management Console.

2. **Configure the environment**: Install TensorFlow and necessary dependencies on the instance:

```bash
pip install tensorflow-gpu
```

3. **Run the training**: Upload your TensorFlow code to the instance and start training.

2.3 Amazon S3 for Data Storage

Amazon S3 is a scalable storage service that can be used to store training data, models, and checkpoints.

Using S3 for Preprocessing and Saving:

```python
import boto3

# Load data from S3
s3 = boto3.client('s3')
s3.download_file('my-bucket', 'data.csv', 'local_data.csv')

# Save a model to S3
```

```
model.save('model.h5')

s3.upload_file('model.h5', 'my-bucket', 'model/model.h5')
```

3. Cloud Machine Learning Services

In addition to compute and storage services, there are various cloud services dedicated specifically to machine learning that can simplify the process of training, evaluating, and deploying models. These services offer integrated solutions to manage the entire ML model lifecycle.

3.1 Google Cloud AI Platform

In addition to training functionality, Google Cloud

AI Platform also offers tools for inference,

model analysis, and ML workflow orchestration.

Model Deployment:

After training the model on AI Platform, you can deploy it for inference using AI Platform Prediction:

```bash
gcloud ai-platform models create my_model --regions us-central1

gcloud ai-platform versions create v1 \
--model=my_model \
--origin=gs://my_bucket/my_model_dir \
--runtime-version=2.4 \
--framework=tensorflow
```

Inference:

Use the REST API to send inference requests to the deployed model:

```python
import google.auth
from googleapiclient import discovery

# Authentication and service creation
credentials, _ = google.auth.default()
service = discovery.build('ml', 'v1', credentials=credentials)

# Send data for inference
request = service.projects().predict(
    name='projects/my-project/models/my_model/versions/v1',
    body={'instances': [{'input': [1, 2, 3, 4]}]}
)
response = request.execute()
print(response)
```

3.2 Amazon SageMaker Autopilot

SageMaker Autopilot is a service that automates the building of ML models, simplifying the entire machine learning process from data preparation to model optimization.

Using SageMaker Autopilot:

1. **Upload data to S3 and start an Autopilot job:**

```python
from sagemaker import get_execution_role
from sagemaker.autopilot import AutoMLJob

role = get_execution_role()
autopilot = AutoMLJob(
    role=role,
```

        input_data='s3://my-bucket/train-data',

    output_data='s3://my-bucket/autopilot-results'

)

    autopilot.run()
    ```


2. **Analyze the results:**

   Autopilot will automatically generate a model and provide performance metrics. You can view the results and choose the best model to deploy.


#### 3.3 Microsoft Azure Machine Learning

Microsoft Azure offers Azure Machine Learning, a platform that includes tools for designing, training, and deploying models. Azure ML supports TensorFlow and also provides tools for model optimization and workflow orchestration.
    ```

Example of Using Azure ML:

1. **Configure a workspace and experiment:**

```python
from azureml.core import Workspace, Experiment
ws = Workspace.from_config()
experiment = Experiment(workspace=ws, name='my-experiment')
```

2. **Run the training:**

Use a custom training environment and define your training scripts as you would locally:

```python
from azureml.core import ScriptRunConfig, Environment
```

```
env = Environment.from_conda_specification(name='myenv', file_path='conda_dependencies.yml')

src = ScriptRunConfig(source_directory='.', script='train.py', environment=env)

run = experiment.submit(config=src)

run.wait_for_completion()
```

3. **Deploy the model:**

After training, you can deploy the model on Azure Kubernetes Service (AKS) for inference:

```python
from azureml.core.model import Model

model = Model.register(workspace=ws, model_path='model.h5', model_name='my_model')

service = Model.deploy(workspace=ws, name='my-service', models=[model],
```

```
    deployment_config=aks_config)
    service.wait_for_deployment()
```

Conclusion

Utilizing TensorFlow with cloud services such as Google Cloud, AWS, and Azure offers numerous advantages, including scalability, flexibility, and access to advanced computational resources. These services not only simplify the training and deployment of machine learning models but also provide advanced tools for monitoring, optimizing, and orchestrating machine learning pipelines. Leveraging cloud capabilities allows developers to focus more on innovation and modeling, leaving infrastructure and resource management to cloud service providers.

7. Practical Examples and Applications in TensorFlow

TensorFlow is a powerful and flexible library for machine learning and deep learning, widely used to develop and implement complex models. In this article, we will explore four practical projects that illustrate the use of TensorFlow in various application domains:

1. **Image Classification**

2. **Natural Language Processing (NLP)**

3. **Time Series Forecasting**

4. **Reinforcement Learning**

Each project will be described in detail, with sample code to demonstrate how TensorFlow can be used to solve real-world problems.

---

1. Image Classification Project

Image classification is a common task in machine learning where the goal is to identify and classify objects or scenes in images. In this example, we will build an image classification model using the CIFAR-10 dataset, which contains 60,000 color images divided into 10 categories.

1.1 Data Preparation

First, let's load and prepare the CIFAR-10 dataset.

```python
import tensorflow as tf
from tensorflow.keras.datasets import cifar10
from tensorflow.keras.utils import to_categorical

# Load the dataset
```

```
(x_train, y_train), (x_test, y_test) = cifar10.load_data()

# Normalize the data
x_train, x_test = x_train / 255.0, x_test / 255.0

# Convert labels to one-hot encoding
y_train = to_categorical(y_train, 10)
y_test = to_categorical(y_test, 10)
```

1.2 Model Construction

We will use a convolutional neural network (CNN) for image classification. CNNs are particularly effective for handling images due to their ability to extract spatial features from the data.

```python
```

```python
from tensorflow.keras.models import Sequential
from tensorflow.keras.layers import Conv2D, MaxPooling2D, Flatten, Dense

# Define the model
model = Sequential([
    Conv2D(32, (3, 3), activation='relu', input_shape=(32, 32, 3)),
    MaxPooling2D((2, 2)),
    Conv2D(64, (3, 3), activation='relu'),
    MaxPooling2D((2, 2)),
    Conv2D(64, (3, 3), activation='relu'),
    Flatten(),
    Dense(64, activation='relu'),
    Dense(10, activation='softmax')
])

# Compile the model
```

```python
model.compile(optimizer='adam',
              loss='categorical_crossentropy',
              metrics=['accuracy'])
```

1.3 Model Training

Train the model using the prepared data.

```python
# Train the model
history = model.fit(x_train, y_train, epochs=10, batch_size=64, validation_split=0.2)


# Evaluate the model
test_loss, test_acc = model.evaluate(x_test, y_test)
print(f"Test accuracy: {test_acc:.4f}")
```

```

#### 1.4 Inference and Visualization

After training, we can use the model to make predictions on new images and visualize the results.

```python
import matplotlib.pyplot as plt
import numpy as np

# Function to visualize predictions
def plot_predictions(images, labels, predictions):
    fig, axes = plt.subplots(1, len(images), figsize=(15, 5))
    for img, label, pred, ax in zip(images, labels, predictions, axes):
        ax.imshow(img)

```
        ax.axis('off')
        true_label = np.argmax(label)
        predicted_label = np.argmax(pred)
        ax.set_title(f"True: {true_label}, Pred: {predicted_label}")

# Select some test images
images = x_test[:5]
labels = y_test[:5]
predictions = model.predict(images)

# Display predictions
plot_predictions(images, labels, predictions)
plt.show()
```

---

2. Natural Language Processing (NLP) Project

Natural Language Processing (NLP) is a field of machine learning dedicated to understanding and generating human language. In this example, we will build a text classification model using the IMDB dataset, which contains movie reviews labeled as positive or negative.

2.1 Data Preparation

Load and preprocess the IMDB dataset for training our model.

```python
from tensorflow.keras.datasets import imdb
from tensorflow.keras.preprocessing.sequence import pad_sequences
```

```python
# Load the dataset
(x_train, y_train), (x_test, y_test) = imdb.load_data(num_words=10000)

# Padding sequences to standardize length
x_train = pad_sequences(x_train, maxlen=200)
x_test = pad_sequences(x_test, maxlen=200)
```

2.2 Model Construction

We will use a sequential neural network with embedding and LSTM for text classification.

```python
from tensorflow.keras.models import Sequential
from tensorflow.keras.layers import Embedding, LSTM, Dense
```

```
# Define the model
model = Sequential([
    Embedding(10000, 128, input_length=200),
    LSTM(64),
    Dense(1, activation='sigmoid')
])


# Compile the model
model.compile(optimizer='adam',
        loss='binary_crossentropy',
        metrics=['accuracy'])
```

2.3 Model Training

Train the model with the training data and evaluate its performance on the test data.

```python
# Train the model
history = model.fit(x_train, y_train, epochs=5, batch_size=64, validation_split=0.2)

# Evaluate the model
test_loss, test_acc = model.evaluate(x_test, y_test)
print(f"Test accuracy: {test_acc:.4f}")
```

2.4 Inference

Make predictions on new reviews.

```python
# Function to make predictions
def predict_review(review):
    # Preprocess the review
```

```
    review_seq = pad_sequences([review], maxlen=200)

    prediction = model.predict(review_seq)

    return "Positive" if prediction[0] > 0.5 else "Negative"


# Test the model with a new review

review = [1, 2, 3, 4, ...]  # sequence of words converted to numbers

print(predict_review(review))
```

---

3. Time Series Forecasting Project

Time series forecasting is an application of machine learning that predicts future values of a temporal data sequence. We will use a daily temperature dataset to forecast future temperatures.

3.1 Data Preparation

Load and prepare the data for time series forecasting.

```python
import numpy as np
import pandas as pd

# Load the temperature dataset
data = pd.read_csv('temperature_data.csv')

# Create a dataset window for forecasting
def create_dataset(data, look_back=1):
    X, y = [], []
    for i in range(len(data) - look_back):
```

```python
        X.append(data[i:(i + look_back), 0])
        y.append(data[i + look_back, 0])
    return np.array(X), np.array(y)

look_back = 7
data_values = data['temperature'].values
data_values = data_values.reshape(-1, 1)

X, y = create_dataset(data_values, look_back)
X = X.reshape((X.shape[0], X.shape[1], 1))  # [samples, timesteps, features]
```

3.2 Model Construction

Build an LSTM neural network for time series forecasting.

```python
```

```python
from tensorflow.keras.models import Sequential
from tensorflow.keras.layers import LSTM, Dense

# Define the model
model = Sequential([
    LSTM(50, input_shape=(look_back, 1)),
    Dense(1)
])

# Compile the model
model.compile(optimizer='adam', loss='mean_squared_error')
```

3.3 Model Training

Train the model on the time series data.

```python
# Train the model
history = model.fit(X, y, epochs=10, batch_size=1, verbose=2)

# Evaluate the model
test_loss = model.evaluate(X, y)
print(f"Test loss: {test_loss:.4f}")
```

3.4 Forecasting

Make forecasts on future data.

```python
# Forecast with the trained model
predictions = model.predict(X)
```

```python
# Visualize the forecasts
plt.plot(range(len(y)), y, label='True Data')
plt.plot(range(len(predictions)), predictions, label='Predictions')
plt.legend()
plt.show()
```

---

4. Reinforcement Learning Project

Reinforcement learning (RL) is a type of machine learning where an agent learns to make decisions by interacting with an environment. In this example, we will use TensorFlow to build an RL agent that plays a simple game, such as CartPole.

4.1 Environment Setup

We will use the CartPole environment from OpenAI Gym to train our agent.

```python
import gym

# Create the environment
env = gym.make('CartPole-v1')
```

4.2 DQN Model Construction

We will use a Deep Q-Network (DQN) model for the RL agent.

```python
from tensorflow.keras.models import import
```

Sequential

from tensorflow.keras.layers import Dense

from tensorflow.keras.optimizers import Adam

```python
# Define the DQN model
model = Sequential([
    Dense(24, input_shape=(env.observation_space.shape[0],), activation='relu'),
    Dense(24, activation='relu'),
    Dense(env.action_space.n, activation='linear')
])

# Compile the model
model.compile(optimizer=Adam(learning_rate=0.001), loss='mean_squared_error')
```
```
```

4.3 Agent Training

Train the agent using an exploration and exploitation strategy.

```python
import numpy as np
from collections import deque
import random

# Parameters
n_episodes = 1000
max_steps = 200

batch_size = 64
gamma = 0.99
```

```python
# Experience replay
experience_replay = deque(maxlen=2000)


def train_dqn():
    for episode in range(n_episodes):
        state = env.reset()
        state = np.reshape(state, [1,
env.observation_space.shape[0]])
        total_reward = 0

        for step in range(max_steps):
            # Select an action
            if np.random.rand() <= 0.1:
                action = env.action_space.sample()
            else:
                q_values = model.predict(state)
                action = np.argmax(q_values[0])
```

```python
        # Perform the action
        next_state, reward, done, _ = env.step(action)
        next_state = np.reshape(next_state, [1, env.observation_space.shape[0]])
        experience_replay.append((state, action, reward, next_state, done))


        state = next_state
        total_reward += reward


        if len(experience_replay) > batch_size:
            minibatch = random.sample(experience_replay, batch_size)
            for s, a, r, ns, d in minibatch:
                q_values = model.predict(s)
                target = r
                if not d:
                    target += gamma *
```

```
            np.amax(model.predict(ns)[0])
                q_values[0][a] = target
                model.fit(s, q_values, verbose=0)

        if done:
            break

    print(f"Episode: {episode + 1}, Total Reward: {total_reward}")

train_dqn()
```

4.4 Agent Evaluation

After training, we can evaluate the agent's performance.

```python
```

```python
def evaluate_agent():
    total_rewards = 0
    n_evaluations = 10

    for _ in range(n_evaluations):
        state = env.reset()
        state = np.reshape(state, [1, env.observation_space.shape[0]])
        total_reward = 0

        for _ in range(max_steps):
            q_values = model.predict(state)
            action = np.argmax(q_values[0])
            next_state, reward, done, _ = env.step(action)
            next_state = np.reshape(next_state, [1, env.observation_space.shape[0]])
            state = next_state
            total_reward += reward
```

```
        if done:
            break

    total_rewards += total_reward

print(f"Average Reward: {total_rewards / n_evaluations:.2f}")

evaluate_agent()
```

These examples illustrate how TensorFlow can be used to tackle a variety of real-world problems in machine learning and deep learning. Image classification, natural language processing, time series forecasting, and reinforcement learning are all areas where TensorFlow demonstrates its power and flexibility. Each project involves different techniques and approaches, but TensorFlow provides the necessary tools to build, train, and deploy complex models with ease.

8. Glossary of Key Terms in TensorFlow

TensorFlow is one of the most comprehensive and advanced machine learning libraries available, developed by Google. Its extensive range of features and modular approach can be complex for newcomers. To navigate the world of TensorFlow effectively, it's essential to understand some key terms and fundamental concepts. This glossary explores the most important TensorFlow terms, providing detailed explanations and practical examples.

1. Tensors

Definition

Tensors are the fundamental data structures in TensorFlow. They are multidimensional arrays that can contain data of various types (e.g., integers, floating-point numbers, strings). Tensors are similar to NumPy arrays but with additional dimensions for distributed computation and support for

GPU/TPU.

Example

```python
import tensorflow as tf

# Create a scalar tensor
scalar = tf.constant(5)

# Create a vector tensor
vector = tf.constant([1, 2, 3, 4])

# Create a matrix tensor
matrix = tf.constant([[1, 2], [3, 4]])

# Create a three-dimensional tensor
tensor_3d = tf.constant([[[1], [2]], [[3], [4]]])
```

2. Graphs

Definition

A **graph** in TensorFlow represents a set of mathematical operations and relationships between variables and tensors. TensorFlow uses graphs to optimize and parallelize computation operations.

Example

```python
# Create a simple graph
a = tf.constant(5)
b = tf.constant(3)
c = tf.add(a, b)

with tf.Session() as sess:
    result = sess.run(c)
```

```
    print(result)  # Output: 8
```

3. Sessions

Definition

A **session** is an execution environment in TensorFlow where graphs are run. Sessions execute the operations defined in the graph and return results.

Example

```python
# Define operations
a = tf.constant(5)
b = tf.constant(3)
c = tf.add(a, b)

# Execute operations in a session
```

```python
with tf.Session() as sess:
    result = sess.run(c)
    print(result)  # Output: 8
```

4. Variables

Definition

Variables are tensors whose values can be changed during model training. Variables are often used to store weights and biases in machine learning models.

Example

```python
# Create a variable
variable = tf.Variable(tf.zeros([2, 2]))

# Initialize the variable
```

```
init = tf.global_variables_initializer()

with tf.Session() as sess:
    sess.run(init)
    print(sess.run(variable))
```

5. Placeholders

Definition

Placeholders are tensors without initial values that are used to insert data into TensorFlow graphs during execution. Actual data is provided through feeds during the session.

Example
```python
# Define a placeholder
```

```python
x = tf.placeholder(tf.float32, shape=[None, 2])

# Define an operation
y = tf.multiply(x, 2)

with tf.Session() as sess:
    # Execute the operation with actual data
    result = sess.run(y, feed_dict={x: [[1, 2], [3, 4]]})
    print(result)  # Output: [[2. 4.] [6. 8.]]
```

6. Layers

Definition

Layers are fundamental components in building deep learning models. Each layer processes data differently and may consist of various operations, such as convolutions, activations, and pooling.

Example

```python
from tensorflow.keras.layers import Dense

# Define a model with a dense layer
model = tf.keras.Sequential([
    Dense(64, activation='relu', input_shape=(784,)),
    Dense(10, activation='softmax')
])
```

7. Optimizers

Definition

Optimizers are algorithms used to update model weights during training, minimizing the loss function. Common examples include

SGD, Adam, and RMSprop.

Example

```python
from tensorflow.keras.optimizers import Adam

# Define an optimizer
optimizer = Adam(learning_rate=0.001)

# Compile the model with the optimizer
model.compile(optimizer=optimizer, loss='categorical_crossentropy', metrics=['accuracy'])
```

8. Loss Functions

Definition

Loss functions measure the error between model predictions and actual values. The loss function guides the optimization of model weights.

Example

```python
from tensorflow.keras.losses import SparseCategoricalCrossentropy

# Define a loss function
loss_fn = SparseCategoricalCrossentropy()

# Compile the model with the loss function
model.compile(optimizer='adam', loss=loss_fn, metrics=['accuracy'])
```

9. Metrics

Definition

Metrics are used to evaluate model performance during training and evaluation. Examples include accuracy, precision, recall, and F1-score.

Example

```python
from tensorflow.keras.metrics import Accuracy

# Define a metric
accuracy_metric = Accuracy()

# Compile the model with the metric
model.compile(optimizer='adam', loss='sparse_categorical_crossentropy', metrics=[accuracy_metric])
```

10. Callbacks

Definition

Callbacks are functions that are called during the training process to perform operations like saving models, monitoring metrics, or early stopping.

Example

```python
from tensorflow.keras.callbacks import EarlyStopping, ModelCheckpoint

# Define callbacks for early stopping and model checkpointing
early_stopping = EarlyStopping(monitor='val_loss', patience=3)
model_checkpoint = ModelCheckpoint('model.h5', save_best_only=True)
```

```python
# Train the model with callbacks
model.fit(x_train, y_train, epochs=10, validation_data=(x_test, y_test), callbacks=[early_stopping, model_checkpoint])
```

11. Activation Functions

Definition

Activation functions determine whether a neuron should be activated or not, adding non-linearity to the model. Common functions include ReLU, Sigmoid, and Tanh.

Example

```python
from tensorflow.keras.layers import Activation
```

```
# Apply the ReLU activation function
x = tf.constant([[-1.0, 2.0], [-3.0, 4.0]])
relu = Activation('relu')
result = relu(x)
print(result.numpy())  # Output: [[0. 2.] [0. 4.]]
```

12. Dropout

Definition

Dropout is a regularization technique that prevents overfitting by randomly deactivating a fraction of neurons during training.

Example

```python
from tensorflow.keras.layers import Dropout
```

```python
# Add a dropout layer to the model
model = tf.keras.Sequential([
    Dense(64, activation='relu', input_shape=(784,)),
    Dropout(0.5),
    Dense(10, activation='softmax')
])
```

13. Batch Normalization

Definition

Batch normalization normalizes layer activations during training, improving stability and convergence speed of the model.

Example

```python
from tensorflow.keras.layers import
```

BatchNormalization

```
# Add a batch normalization layer to the model
model = tf.keras.Sequential([
    Dense(64, activation='relu', input_shape=(784,)),
    BatchNormalization(),
    Dense(10, activation='softmax')
])
```

14. Data Pipeline

Definition

Data pipelines are used to manage and preprocess data during training and evaluation. TensorFlow offers the `tf.data` module to build efficient and scalable data pipelines.

Example

```python
import tensorflow as tf

# Create a data pipeline
dataset = tf.data.Dataset.from_tensor_slices((x_train, y_train))
dataset = dataset.shuffle(buffer_size=10000).batch(64).prefetch(tf.data.AUTOTUNE)

# Use the pipeline during training
model.fit(dataset, epochs=10)
```

15. Eager Execution

Definition

Eager Execution is a mode in TensorFlow that executes operations immediately without building a graph. This mode is useful for debugging and interactive operations.

Example

```python
import tensorflow as tf

# Enable eager execution
tf.config.run_functions_eagerly(True)

# Execute operations in eager mode
a = tf.constant(2)
b = tf.constant(3)
c = a + b
print(c.numpy())  # Output: 5
```

```

## 16. SavedModel

### Definition

**SavedModel** is the standard format for saving and loading models in TensorFlow. It includes the model architecture, weights, and configuration information.

### Example

```python
# Save a model
model.save('saved_model/my_model')

# Load a model
loaded_model = tf.keras.models.load_model('saved_model/my_model')
```
```

17. TensorBoard

Definition

TensorBoard is a visualization tool that allows you to monitor and visualize training metrics, model architectures, and other statistics during training.

Example

```python
from tensorflow.keras.callbacks import TensorBoard

# Define the TensorBoard callback
tensorboard_callback = TensorBoard(log_dir='./logs')

# Train the model with TensorBoard
model.fit(x_train, y_train, epochs=10,
```

```
    validation_data=(x_test, y_test),
    callbacks=[tensorboard_callback])

# Start TensorBoard
# tensorboard --logdir=./logs
```

18. tf.function

Definition

tf.function is a decorator that converts a Python function into a TensorFlow graph. This improves performance by making operations more efficient.

Example

```python
@tf.function
def add_tensors(a, b):
```

    return a + b

Execute the function

result = add_tensors(tf.constant(2), tf.constant(3))

print(result.numpy()) # Output: 5
``
`

19. Estimator

Definition

Estimator is a high-level API for building and training models in TensorFlow. It provides easy integration with datasets and pipelines and supports distributed training.

Example

```python
from tensorflow.compat.v1 import Estimator
from tensorflow.compat.v1 import feature_column

# Define an Estimator
def model_fn(features, labels, mode):
    # Define the model
    net = tf.feature_column.input_layer(features, feature_columns)
    net = tf.layers.Dense(10, activation='relu')(net)
    logits = tf.layers.Dense(1)(net)

    # Calculate the loss
    loss = tf.losses.mean_squared_error(labels, logits)

    # Optimizer
```

```
optimizer = tf.train.AdamOptimizer()
train_op = optimizer.minimize(loss, global_step=tf.train.get_global_step())


    return tf.estimator.EstimatorSpec(mode=mode, loss=loss, train_op=train_op)


estimator = Estimator(model_fn=model_fn)
```

20. tf.data

Definition

tf.data is a TensorFlow module for building high-performance input pipelines. It allows you to read, preprocess, and transform data efficiently.

Example

```python
import tensorflow as tf

# Create a sample dataset
dataset = tf.data.Dataset.range(10)
dataset = dataset.map(lambda x: x * 2).batch(2)

# Iterate over the dataset
for batch in dataset:
    print(batch.numpy())  # Output: [0 2], [4 6], [8]
```

21. Hub

Definition

TensorFlow Hub is a library for publishing and sharing pre-trained models. It allows easy and quick reuse of models and components.

Example

```python
import tensorflow_hub as hub

# Load a model from TensorFlow Hub
model = hub.KerasLayer("https://tfhub.dev/google/imagenet/mobilenet_v2_100_224/classification/4")

# Use the model
predictions = model(tf.constant(images))
```

22. Quantization

Definition

Quantization is a technique for reducing the precision of computations and model weights to improve performance and reduce model size without significantly losing precision.

Example

```python
import tensorflow as tf

from tensorflow_model_optimization.sparsity import keras as sparsity

# Create a model
model = tf.keras.Sequential([
    tf.keras.layers.Dense(128, activation='relu', input_shape=(784,)),
    tf.keras.layers.Dense(10, activation='softmax')
])
```

```
# Apply quantization
quant_model = tf.keras.models.clone_model(model, clone_function=tf.quantization.quantize_model)
```

23. TensorFlow Extended (TFX)

Definition

TensorFlow Extended (TFX) is an end-to-end platform for deploying machine learning models. It provides tools for data management, pipeline creation, and production deployment.

Example

```python
# A practical example of using TFX to create a pipeline
```

```
import tfx

# Define a TFX pipeline
pipeline = tfx.dsl.Pipeline(
    pipeline_name='example_pipeline',
    components=[

tfx.components.ExampleGen(input_base='path/to/data'),
        tfx.components.SchemaGen(),
        tfx.components.ExampleValidator(),
        tfx.components.Trainer(),
        tfx.components.Pusher()
    ],
    # Other configuration parameters
)
```
```

## 24. AutoML
```

Definition

AutoML refers to a set of techniques that automate the design and optimization of machine learning models. TensorFlow provides tools like AutoKeras for automatic model creation.

Example

```python
import autokeras as ak

# Create an automatic classification model
model = ak.ImageClassifier(max_trials=10)
model.fit(x_train, y_train, epochs=10)

# Evaluate the model
accuracy = model.evaluate(x_test, y_test)
print(f"Test accuracy: {accuracy:.4f}")
```

```

## 25. Distributed Training

### Definition

**Distributed Training** is a technique for training models across multiple machines or devices to reduce training time and handle large datasets. TensorFlow offers tools for distributing training, such as `tf.distribute.Strategy`.

### Example

```python
import tensorflow as tf

# Define a strategy for distributed training
strategy = tf.distribute.MirroredStrategy()

# Build and train the model with the strategy

```
with strategy.scope():
    model = tf.keras.Sequential([
        tf.keras.layers.Dense(64, activation='relu', input_shape=(784,)),
        tf.keras.layers.Dense(10, activation='softmax')
    ])
    model.compile(optimizer='adam', loss='sparse_categorical_crossentropy', metrics=['accuracy'])
    model.fit(x_train, y_train, epochs=10)
```

This glossary provides a comprehensive overview of key TensorFlow terms and concepts. Understanding these terms is crucial for fully leveraging TensorFlow's capabilities and developing advanced machine learning and deep learning models. By using the definitions and examples provided, you can gain a solid grasp of TensorFlow's main components and functionalities, facilitating the construction and optimization of your models.

Index

1. Introduzione pg.4

2. Fundamentals of Machine Learning in TensorFlow pg.34

3. Data Structures in TensorFlow pg.53

4. Model Building in TensorFlow pg.73

5. Datasets and Preprocessing in TensorFlow pg.93

6. TensorFlow and the Cloud pg.113

7. Practical Examples and Applications in TensorFlow pg.137

8.Glossary of Key Terms in TensorFlow pg.163

www.ingramcontent.com/pod-product-compliance
Lightning Source LLC
Chambersburg PA
CBHW071052240526
45471CB00015B/1664